EPSOM PUBLIC LIBRARY

1893

GREAT EXPLORATIONS

DANIEL BOONE

Beyond the Mountains

PATRICIA CALVERT

BENCHMARK BOOKS

MARSHALL CAVENDISH
NEW YORK

For
Irena Helen Clarkowski—
welcome to the world!

With special thanks to Stephen Pitti, Yale University,
for his careful reading of this manuscript.

JB
BOO

17446

Benchmark Books
Marshall Cavendish Corporation
99 White Plains Road
Tarrytown, New York 10591-9001

Library of Congress Cataloging-in-Publication Data
Calvert, Patricia.
Daniel Boone: Beyond the Mountains by Patricia Calvert
p   cm. – (Great explorations)
Includes bibliographical references ([.) and index.
ISBN 0-7614-1243-3
1. Boone, Daniel, 1734-1820—Juvenile literature. 2. Pioneers—Kentucky—Biography—Juvenile literature.
3. Explorers—Kentucky—Biography—Juvenile literature. 4. Frontier and pioneer life—Kentucky—Juvenile
literature. 5. Kentucky—Biography—Juvenile literature. 6. Kentucky—Discovery and exploration—Juvenile
literature. 7. Missouri—Discovery and exploration—Juvenile literature. [1. Boone, Daniel. 1734-1820. 2. Pioneers.]
I. Title. II. Series.
F454.B66 C35 2001   976.9'02'092—dc21   [B]   00-051902

Photo Research by Candlepants Incorporated
Cover Photo: Art Resource, NY / Smithsonian American Art Museum, Washington DC
Cover Inset : Kentucky Historical Society, Special Collections and Archives
The photographs in this book are used by permission and through the courtesy of; *Art Resource, NY* :
Smithsonian American Art Museum, Washington DC, 4; National Museum of American Art, Washington DC, 48;
Scala, 65. *The Granger Collection* : 6, 56. *Corbis* : 66, 67; Museum of the City of New York, 9; Gianni Dagli Orti, 11;
Bettmann, 13, 15, 17, 20, 23, 25, 35, 45. *Gilcrease Museum, Tulsa* : 27. *Stark Museum of Art* : 28. *Washington
University Gallery of Art, St Louis* : Gift of Nathaniel Phillips, 1890, 31; Transfer from Special Collections,
Olin Library, Washington University, 1988, 41, 43. *Division of Historic Properties, Kentucky State Capitol* : 34.
The Filson Club Historical Society, Louisville, KY : 37, 58. *Olin Library, Washington University, St. Louis* : 52.
The Missouri Historical Society : 61. *Mead Art Museum, Amherst College, Amherst, MA* : 64. *John James
Audubon State Park* : 69.

Printed in Hong Kong
1   3   5   6   4   2

Contents

A portrait of Daniel Boone. The coat Daniel is wearing is like
the one in which he wrapped his son James on winter hunting trips,
"hugging the little fellow closely" to keep them both warm.

foreword

. . . thanks to God for such a peaceful and excellent shelter in the wilderness.

Sir William Penn, 1700

The Boone family came from a long line of freedom seekers. Their Norman ancestors left ninth-century France and sailed west to settle in Devonshire, at the southern tip of England. It would only be the first of many times that the Boones turned their faces westward.

Bradninch, a hamlet near the larger village of Exeter, became home to Daniel's grandfather, George. He was the father of nine children and eked out a precarious living as a weaver. Like many others of the Quaker faith, he dreamed of moving to the New World.

The Quakers, also called the Society of Friends, were pacifists who refused to bear arms, would not swear an oath to the king, and did not believe that priests and ministers needed to act as intermediaries between man and God. As a result, more than 15,000 Quakers had been

Explorers like Daniel Boone opened the door to the West.

sent to prison, where 400 died. Many fled to the New World to escape further persecution.

However, George Boone wanted something besides religious freedom: he wanted *land.* For a poor weaver like himself, there was no chance he could ever own land in England. Yet he knew it would be foolhardy to move his large family to a strange new country without knowing more about the challenges they might face.

In 1712, the weaver finally dispatched his three oldest children to America to take stock of the situation firsthand. George Jr., Sarah, and Squire were to report back to their father what they found. Sixteen-year-old Squire, the youngest of the three, earned his ship's passage by working as a cabin boy. Twenty-two years later, Squire would have a son of his own, a boy named Daniel.

George Boone's children wrote enthusiastic letters to their father about what they discovered in the New World. In 1681, William Penn, a fellow Quaker, had founded Pennsylvania (the name meant "Penn's Woods"), where an acre of land could be rented for a penny a year. A man could hold "as much property as one wishes . . . in summer one can shoot a deer, dress the skin, and wear pants from it in twenty four hour," young George wrote. Sarah and George were also pleased for romantic reasons: Both had met people in American they wished to marry.

As much property as one wishes! The words were music to George Boone's ears, a man who had been hungry for land all his life. He gathered up his wife, Mary, and their six younger children—the youngest two were still so small they made the voyage for half the fare—and the family traveled eighty miles on foot to the port of Bristol. On August 17, 1717, the Boones sailed for the New World.

O N E

Beyond the Mountains

When he was an old man, Daniel Boone liked to entertain his grand-children with yarns from his childhood. His favorite was the story of how he got smallpox when he was four years old.

An epidemic had spread through Oley Township in western Pennsylvania, so mothers kept their children indoors until it passed. Daniel—born on November 2, 1734, the sixth of the Boones' ten children—hated being locked up like a prisoner.

Finally, the boy and his six-year-old sister Elizabeth decided to get the pox and be done with it. But how to catch it?

Remembering that neighbors had gotten it, they crept out at night, ran down the road, and hopped into bed with the sick children, who probably were astonished to have company at such an hour. Daniel and Elizabeth were home before daybreak. A few days later, they showed symptoms of the disease.

A typical pioneer family's home. Daniel Boone probably grew up in a similar setting.

Their mother, Sarah Boone was puzzled. She questioned her son, who admitted what he and Elizabeth had done. Except for a scolding—his mother called him a "gorrel," an English word meaning lout—Daniel wasn't punished. He was her favorite, he remembered, "above all her children."

Sarah was tolerant of Daniel's shenanigans, but his father wasn't. Squire Boone punished his sons for their misdeeds by thrashing them until they asked for forgiveness, then reasoned with them in a gentle Quaker fashion. Such discipline worked with the other boys but not with Daniel, who silently endured his punishment. Squire—who didn't beat his sons because it gave him pleasure—pleaded, "Canst thou not beg?" But Daniel never did.

In 1744, when Daniel was ten, Squire Boone bought twenty-five acres of grazing land five miles (eight kilometers) from the family homestead. Until he was fifteen, Daniel helped his mother take the cows out every summer to graze. They built a hut beside a creek that kept the milk cool until Sarah made it into butter and cheese. Once a week she took the dairy products home to trade to other settlers for shoes, nails, and other essentials.

Daniel went home each week with Sarah, but soon he asked to stay behind and tend the cows by himself. He looked after them haphazardly, because he was more interested in perfecting his hunting skills. He was only ten, too young to be given a rifle, so he fashioned a "herdsman's club" from a sapling. It had a knob on one end (to serve as a handle), and was sharpened to a point on the other. He became expert at hurling this weapon, killing many a rabbit with it.

Although the Quakers were pacifists, they weren't opposed to guns. A rifle was an essential tool for any settler, and when Daniel was twelve or thirteen his father gave him a short-barreled rifle. Soon the boy was supplying his family with all the meat it needed, which meant he never learned much about raising crops. A relative observed, "Daniel was ever unpracticed in the business of farming, but grew up a woodsman and a hunter."

Like other members of the Society of Friends (Quakers), the Boones had left England to enjoy greater religious freedom. Once settled in the New World, however, they discovered that persecution had followed them. This time, it came not from the English Crown, but from the Quakers themselves.

In 1742, Daniel's oldest sister, Sarah, married a "worldling," a man not of the Quaker faith. Worse, it was plain that Sarah was pregnant before she took her vows. Squire Boone had to apologize for his daughter's behavior before a meeting of the Friends. He was warned to "be more Careful for the future" about his children's conduct.

King Charles II of England was pleased when many of the Quakers followed William Penn, also a Quaker, to the New World and settled in Pennsylvania.

Five years later, Daniel's brother Israel also married out. This time, Squire Boone wasn't as quick to apologize. He declared that his family had come to America seeking religious freedom, that it was his son's right to marry whomever he wished. Consequently, Squire was "disowned" by the Society of Friends.

It was the last straw. Daniel's father sold his property and prepared to leave Pennsvylvania. He refused to be persecuted, even by Quakers. Yet as the noted Boone biographer John Bakeless observed, something else was also at work. "The Boones were wanderers born. . . . Something beyond the mountains always whispered."

QUAKERS IN THE NEW WORLD

King Charles II was eager to be rid of all Quakers in England; he believed they were dangerous to established order. In 1681, he awarded 28 million acres of land in the American colonies to William Penn, a Quaker, hoping that many of his kind would follow. In 1682, Penn founded the city of Philadelphia, a name formed from two Greek words, *philos*, meaning "love," and *adelphos*, meaning "brother."

Settlers moved west in wagons pulled by oxen or horses. Cows, pigs, and other live-stock were herded along, sometimes with the help of the family's dog.

By 1750, many colonists had already emigrated to North Carolina. Their reasons had nothing to do with religion. In those days, fields weren't fertilized as they are now, nor were crops rotated to rest the land. Such treatment meant fields wore out quickly. Rather than change their habits, farmers found it was easier to start over with a fresh patch of ground.

Another fact also prompted settlers to move. The steady stream of arrivals from the Old World had thinned the Pennsylvania woods of timber and game. Men had to go farther for firewood and lumber, and hunt longer to bring meat home to their families. Among those who followed the Boones out of Pennsylvania was their friend John Lincoln, Abraham Lincoln's great-grandfather.

On the first of May, 1750, the Boones headed for North Carolina, five hundred miles (eight hundred kilometers) away. They were accom-

panied by two of Daniel's cousins, John and George Boone, and Daniel's friend Henry Miller. Small children were hoisted atop wagons loaded with bedding, pots, pans, and crates of chickens, while older boys and girls herded the cattle along.

Fifteen-year-old Daniel carried a long rifle in place of the short-barreled kind of his early years, and went ahead with the men. He may have been young—a slender, blue-eyed boy, not especially tall for his age—but he was already respected for his hunting skills and knowledge of the woods.

The Boones camped a long time in Virginia, arriving in North Carolina around 1752. Daniel's friend Henry Miller was satisfied with what he found in Virginia, and stayed there. Years later, one of Miller's descendants said that Henry decided to "settle down, make money, and keep it." When the two friends met thirty years later, Henry had become the founder of the first ironworks in Virginia and was well-off indeed. Daniel Boone was penniless—but it's his name that went into the history books.

When the Boones arrived in North Carolina, 25,000 other immigrants had already settled there. The fewest were in the Yadkin Valley, on the western border of the colony, and that's where the Boones headed. The family spent their first winter in a cave. Then, in April 1753, Squire bought 640 acres along Buffalo Creek, and later an additional 640 on the west side of the Yadkin Valley.

Work began on a proper home that today would be considered rustic: a single-room log dwelling about twenty feet (six meters) square. Its roof was steeply pitched to shed rain and snow. Inside, a curtain was pulled across to section off a sleeping area. A stone fireplace provided heat and a place to cook.

Felling trees and clearing land occupied the men, including Daniel.

Forests needed to be cleared in the New World. Settlers used the logs to build their cabins and to provide wood for heat.

But when the weather turned sour, making it hard to do such work, Daniel returned to the pastime he loved best: hunting. A good marksman could take as many as thirty deer a day. The meat was made into jerky by drying over a low fire; the hides were sold for cash.

Eighty-year-old Morgan Bryan, a prosperous fellow Quaker and head of a large family, also lived in the Yadkin Valley. In 1754, Daniel's younger sister Mary married William Bryan. At the wedding, young Daniel's eye was caught by one of old Morgan's pretty granddaughters, fifteen-year-old Rebecca. He was smitten, and although the two were too shy to speak on that occasion, Daniel was tempted to begin courting her then and there. A war loomed on the horizon, however, and he postponed his plans.

T W O

Sheep before the Hounds

England and France both claimed ownership of the North Carolina region where the Boones had settled. The British based their claim on the Virginia charter of 1609; the French cited René-Robert Cavalier, Sieur de La Salle's 1669 exploration of the Ohio River to support theirs.

The French were mainly interested in developing their lucrative fur trade, while the English dreamed of a colonial empire based on the timber, coal, and agriculture of the area. Both, however, enlisted Indians to fight on their side.

Because the French were interested in furs, not in establishing settlements, they left the Indians free to pursue their traditional way of life. By contrast, the English built forts and villages in the heart of the best Indian hunting grounds, pushing the natives aside. As a result, many tribes aligned themselves with the French, and so began what were called the Border Wars.

The Indians often traded furs with other tribes. When whites came
to the New World, they began to trade with them, as well.

The British governor of Virginia, alarmed by Indian attacks on colonists in North Carolina, dispatched the militia under the command of a twenty-one-year-old major to warn the French that their recruitment of Indians would mean war. The young man, the son of a wealthy Virginia planter, was only two years older than Daniel Boone. His name was George Washington.

In 1754, after the Shawnees killed thirteen people and took ten others prisoner at Buffalo Creek, near Boone's home, Daniel signed up with the North Carolina militia and rode off to war.

In 1755, the British sent General Edward Braddock to take command of both the colonial militia and the British regulars. Braddock, fresh from England, had no experience in forest warfare. Young Washington, now a lieutenant colonel, warned the general about the danger of fighting a European-style war in the wilderness—that is, of marching soldiers in orderly columns to confront an enemy who met one's forces in the same way. Braddock dismissed Washington's advice, accusing the militia of having "little courage and no good will."

Then, instead of traveling light with packhorses, Braddock commandeered one hundred fifty cumbersome wagons from local settlers, along with five hundred draft horses to pull them. The wagons were heavily loaded with supplies, and the general proceeded noisily toward Fort Duquesne, the French outpost overlooking present-day Pittsburgh.

The excitement of war was infectious, and Daniel was pleased with his job as a wagoner. However, he soon heard stories around evening campfires that stirred him more than war. He listened raptly as John Findley, a fellow wagoner and one of the first white men to explore what is now Tennessee and Kentucky, spun yarn after yarn.

According to Findley, corn and grain grew in that country practically without attention. The woods were so rich with game that a man hardly needed to hunt because bear and deer could be shot from his doorstep. Beaver, mink, and otter could be trapped in great numbers.

So many fish filled the streams that a man could scoop them out with a frying pan.

In spite of Washington's warnings, early in the morning on July 9, 1755, General Braddock marched his men boldly forward in traditional European style. They approached Fort Duquesne, "colors flying, drums beating, and fifes playing...their burnished arms gleaming in the bright summer's sun." In the afternoon, after Boone and the other wagoners had forded the Monongahela River, they were suddenly fired upon by French troops and 800 Indians waiting in ambush.

Braddock ordered the wagoners not to retreat, but when some British regulars fled past "like sheep before the hounds" (in Washington's words), Boone and other wagoners cut the traces of their teams and galloped to safety on their lead horses. It would be fourteen years before Daniel met John Findley again.

Braddock, still heedless of Washington's warnings, ordered the remainder of his regulars into columns, their red coats making them easy targets for the French and Indians. In three hours on that summer afternoon, 714 British soldiers and 26 officers were killed, including the haughty Braddock himself.

When he was mustered out of the militia, Daniel hurried home to court the girl who'd been on his mind since he met her at his sister's wedding. He saw Rebecca Bryan again at a gathering of young people, where she appeared wearing a fine white apron, a luxurious item in those days. No sketches or portraits exist of Rebecca, so historians can't say for sure what she looked like. Comments from family members describe her as taller than average, dark-haired and dark-eyed, suggesting that she may have looked rather like Daniel's mother, Sarah.

It was the custom for a young man to bring a deer to the doorstep of his betrothed, then skin it and butcher it in her presence to demon-

Against George Washington's advice, General Braddock marched against the Indians. As a result, he lost more than seven hundred of his men, as well as his own life.

strate his ability to provide for a family. Daniel considered the deed a pleasure, not a chore. On August 14, 1756, a year after Braddock's defeat, the couple were married and settled in a small cabin near Daniel's family.

Daniel once joked that all a man needed for happiness was "a good gun, a good horse, and a good wife." His union with Rebecca lasted until her death fifty-seven years later. If she objected to being ranked third on her husband's list, there's no record that she said so.

THREE

The Skeleton in a Hollow Tree

Daniel and Rebecca had scarcely said "I do" when they found themselves with two small children to raise. Daniel's older brother Israel died of consumption (tuberculosis), as did his wife and two daughters, leaving sons Jesse and Jonathan orphans. The boys came to live with the newlyweds, and stayed for seventeen years.

The Boones' first baby, James, was born nine months later. In less than two years a second son, Israel, arrived. Before she was twenty, Rebecca Boone was the mother of four little boys. It isn't surprising that she wanted to be nearer her own parents, so Rebecca and Daniel left their cabin on Squire Boone's homestead and moved several miles away to Sugartree Creek, close to present-day Farmington, North Carolina.

Daniel set about building a house for a family that never stopped growing. In all, he and Rebecca had ten children of their own (one died

BOONE'S CHILDREN

James, born May 3, 1757
Israel, born January 25, 1759
Susannah, born November 2, 1760
Jemima, born October 4, 1762
Levina, born March 23, 1766
Rebecca, born May 26, 1768
Daniel, born December 23, 1769
Jesse, born May 23, 1773
William, born June 1775 (died in infancy)
Nathan, born March 2, 1781

in infancy), and raised two of Daniel's nephews, plus six orphans left by Rebecca's brother.

Daniel took up "scratch" farming—raising only enough to feed his own family, with little left to be sold or traded. As always, hunting and trapping occupied most of his time. He sold the hides and pelts for cash, which enabled him to buy necessities such as flour, sugar, and tea, and to pay his taxes.

The battle at Fort Duquesne didn't end the conflict between the British and the French, who continued using Indians to fight their battles for them. After Fort Dobbs was attacked by a large force of Cherokees in February 1760, Rebecca declared she'd had enough. Daniel's parents had already fled to safety in Virginia. With his own family, as well as those of his sister Elizabeth and his brother Edward—

Men of the frontier needed to be expert marksmen. Gunpowder was too precious to be wasted, either when hunting game or when fighting an enemy.

called Ned by the family—Daniel headed for the tobacco-growing country near Culpeper, Virginia, two hundred miles (320 kilometers) away.

There was safety in Culpeper, but Daniel hated it. City life wasn't to his liking. After Rebecca gave birth to their first daughter, Susannah—on Daniel's twenty-sixth birthday—he asked Ned to take care of his family. (Ned looked enough like Daniel to be his twin.) Daniel lit out for the woods, going first to the North Carolina backcountry to hunt and trap, then on to eastern Tennessee and southwestern Virginia.

Boone and men like him were accused by preachers of the day of wanting to live more like Indians than white men, of not providing for their wives and children. In Boone's case, the life of a hunter and trapper fit him like a comfortable old coat. From boyhood onward, he considered the woods his natural home—and being married didn't change him.

Yet long separations between husband and wife could have poignant results. When Daniel returned to Culpeper in 1762, having been gone almost two years, Rebecca greeted him with a new baby in her arms.

Daniel realized the child, a daughter named Jemima, could not be his. Rebecca wept, explaining that during his absence she had turned to Ned for companionship. "Dry up your tears," Boone said, and took the baby as his own.

Daniel moved his family back to their home on Sugartree Creek in North Carolina in November 1762. But as settlers flooded the region, it became harder to harvest furs and hides, which had been the only way he could earn enough cash to pay his taxes and the creditors to whom he owed money for things he didn't raise himself. In 1764, he was sued for an unpaid debt. The same year, he moved his family farther up the Yadkin Valley toward the Brushy Mountains, hoping to find more game.

Daniel Boone, like other men of the frontier, wore deerskin shirts and leggings. Such garments wore well and could be easily replaced.

A year later, Squire Boone died at age sixty-nine. The death of his father helped Daniel sever his attachment to the Yadkin Valley. He suggested to Rebecca that the family move to the Blue Ridge Mountains, where he knew hunting and trapping were excellent. She refused. Life was hard enough with kinfolk nearby; it would only be worse in such an isolated setting.

But Daniel's feet were itchy. In August 1765, in the company of Major John Field, four other friends, his younger brother Squire, and his brother-in-law John Stewart, he set out to explore Florida, five hundred miles (eight hundred kilometers) away. Two years earlier the territory had been ceded to Britain by Spain. To lure people to the area, the British promised one hundred acres of free land to each Protestant settler.

As far as Daniel was concerned, Florida's main attraction—more powerful than free land—was the prospect of plentiful game. What the men found instead was miles of swamp, alligators lying in the water like submerged logs, and mosquitoes by the millions. Yet when Daniel got home on Christmas Day 1765, he told Rebecca he'd accepted his free acres. Again, she refused to move.

To Daniel's delight, the winter of 1768 brought an old friend to his doorstep. John Findley, his fellow wagoner in Braddock's War, arrived at Sugartree Creek. He'd become an Indian trader, and had explored the wilderness of *Kan-ta-ke*, an Iroquois word meaning "place of fields."

Findley told stories of a secret passage—he called it a "gap"—through the Cumberland Mountains. The passage led to the Warrior's Path, used by the Cherokees for raids against the Shawnees. But Findley didn't know exactly where it was; he needed a guide to help him find it.

He'd come to the right man. In the spring of 1769, Daniel set out with Findley, John Stewart (his sister Hannah's husband), and several

Daniel Boone's first glimpse of Kentucky—the Iroquois called it <u>Kan-ta-ke</u>, or "the place of fields"—revealed a country that was everything he'd dreamed it would be.

other men to search for the secret passage. Daniel found what *he* was looking for in Kentucky: Deer were abundant, so he and Stewart immediately set about hunting them. The hide of a buck weighed about two pounds (one kilogram) and was worth a dollar. To this day, we refer to a dollar as "a buck."

Boone also found the notch in the mountains that became a gateway to the west, the Cumberland Gap. But this was Indian country, and the Shawnees didn't take the intrusion of whites lightly. They raided Boone's camp and took all the hides and furs that he and Stewart had collected. The two men were captured, but managed to escape into the tangled canebrake, where even angry Shawnees wouldn't go.

Men and women on the frontier were always alert to the danger around them. Indians resented the intrusion of settlers into their favorite hunting grounds and often took strong action against the whites.

When the two hunters got back to camp, they discovered that Findley and the others were gone. But Daniel and Stewart were loath to go home empty-handed. It was winter, the ideal time to trap beaver and otter, whose fur would be in prime condition. Beaver pelts were worth about two dollars each, otter about three to five dollars. They knew that, with a fresh harvest of deerskins as well, they could still turn a profit.

Daniel and his brother-in-law agreed to split up, each man working a separate area, and meet every two weeks at their original camp. But John Stewart was never seen again. Daniel searched for him, even came across a cold campfire and the initials *J.S.* carved on a nearby tree, but his sister's husband—the father of four children—had vanished.

Five years passed before the mystery was solved. While Daniel was supervising the building of the Wilderness Road in 1775, a woodcutter found a man's bones in a hollow tree several miles from Stewart's final camp. A powder horn concealed with the skeleton bore his initials, and a closer inspection showed that Stewart had taken a bullet in his left arm. He had probably been attacked by Indians and hidden inside the tree, where he bled to death.

In spite of his partner's disappearance, Boone continued to hunt, trap, and explore Kentucky and Ohio. For a while his younger brother Squire joined him, and they amassed a second harvest of skins and furs. As they started for home in March 1771, however, another Indian raid wiped out what they'd accumulated—about 1,500 hides and pelts.

The loss meant that when Daniel got home after an absence of two years he was nearly penniless. He was deeper in debt than ever. Yet in a sense he was rich, for he knew as much about the unexplored territory of Kentucky and Ohio as any white man alive.

F O U R

A Dark Cloud Over the Country

After Daniel met Captain William Russell, a pioneer in Kentucky's Clinch Valley, he became more determined than ever to move. When he was sued by a lawyer named Richard Henderson for nonpayment of debt and a warrant was issued for his arrest, Daniel decided he'd have a better chance of settling with his creditors if he could make a fresh start somewhere else.

But he worried that the best land in "the place of fields" would be taken if he didn't stake a claim soon. He was so insistent about opportunities in Kentucky that Rebecca and several of her relatives finally agreed to join him. So did his brother Squire, his wife, Jane, and their three sons. Jesse and Jonathan, Daniel's nephews, were ready to start lives of their own and stayed behind.

When Daniel said farewell to his mother, the two clung to each

Daniel Boone Escorting Settlers Through The Cumberland Gap by George Caleb Bingham.

other and wept, realizing they'd probably never see each other again. (Sarah died four years later.)

In September 1773, after Rebecca had recovered from the birth of her eighth child, the group traveled to Castle's Woods to join Captain Russell. Daniel's oldest son, James, was now sixteen and had been hunting with his father since he was eight years old. On cold nights, Boone recalled, he had wrapped the boy in the folds of his own coat, "hugging the little fellow closely to his bosom" to keep them both warm.

The journey west was arduous, the trail so narrow that horses were ridden along it single file. Then, at dawn on October 9, 1773, as James was accompanying a supply party three miles (five kilometers) behind the main group, it was attacked by Indians. James and young Henry Russell, the captain's son, were each shot through the hip, making it impossible for them to escape.

Adam, one of Captain Russell's slaves, was luckier. He hid in the woods and saw what happened next. James recognized one of the Indians—an acquaintance of his father named Big Jim—and pleaded for his life. No mercy was granted. The boys were tortured horribly until they begged to die.

When news of the murders reached James's parents, Rebecca found linen sheets to wrap the boys in for burial. "James was a good son," Daniel said later, "and I looked forward to a long and useful life for him, but it is not to be."

The deaths discouraged the other emigrants, who turned back to safer settlements in Virginia and North Carolina. But the Boones had nothing to return to; they had sold their land back home. An empty cabin at Castle's Woods was offered to them, and they settled down to face a heartbroken winter. James's death was "the worst melancholy of my life," Daniel admitted.

In June 1774, a new challenge took Daniel's mind off his sorrow. A party of surveyors had been sent to Kentucky by the British governor of Virginia, Lord Dunmore, who was eager to acquire land in Kentucky's bluegrass country (bluegrass is a tall-stemmed, bluish-colored wild hay that covered many Kentucky meadows and provided excellent pasture for horses and cattle). As tensions increased between Indians and whites, placing the surveyors in danger, Dunmore realized they must be warned and brought back. Captain Russell recommended "two of the best Hands I could think of, Danl Boone, and Michl Stoner" to search for the men.

Michael Stoner became one of Daniel's closest friends. An orphan, he'd left Pennsylvania at age sixteen, and was called one of the best shots in Kentucky. The pair set out. But, before they could reach the surveyors, two of them were killed. The others had split into smaller groups and headed east. Not until August 26 did Boone and Stoner locate one of the groups and led the men back to Castle's Woods. The rescuers had covered eight hundred miles (1,300 kilometers) in their search, which taught Daniel even more about Kentucky.

The tension between the settlers and the Indians became known as "Lord Dunmore's War." Daniel was put in command of three hastily built forts in the Clinch Valley—Blackmore's Fort, Moore's Fort, and Russell's Fort—where frightened settlers could be protected. Boone also signed up with the militia; he became a lieutenant, then a captain. The war ended in October 1774, with the surrender of Chief Cornstalk of the Shawnees, and Boone was discharged on November 20.

Back in North Carolina, Richard Henderson, who'd filed suit against Daniel for a bad debt, had hatched a scheme to buy twenty million acres of land from the Cherokees in the present states of Kentucky and Tennessee, where he intended to found a fourteenth American colony called Transylvania.

The fact that North Carolina and Virginia had prior claims to the territory didn't bother Henderson. Nor did the British proclamation of 1763, which forbade private citizens from purchasing land from Indian tribes. Henderson's plot was served well by rumors of a rebellion in the colonies—an American revolution—that kept British officials preoccupied.

Henderson might have continued to press the debt case against Daniel except that no other man knew more about the country he wanted to purchase. No further mention was made of the lawsuit. Instead, Henderson proposed that Boone help negotiate a land deal with the Cherokees and supervise the building of a road into the country for a

Painter T. Gilbert White's depiction of the signing of the Sycamore Shoals Treaty, in the Kentucky state capitol at Frankfort, Kentucky. The treaty was voided later, which meant Daniel Boone didn't receive the prime bluegrass land he'd been promised.

reward of two thousand acres of prime bluegrass land.

Daniel met with Henderson and his associates in March 1775, a few days after the marriage of his oldest daughter, Susannah, to William Hays. Treaty talks were immediately started with a thousand Cherokees at Sycamore Shoals, one of the Indians' favorite meeting grounds.

Toward the end of the talks, Henderson ordered up six wagonloads of gifts for the Indians—guns, blankets, clothing—and of course there was plenty of food and rum to promote a spirit of friendship. The Cherokees thoroughly enjoyed themselves, but they refused to sign a treaty. Boone finally convinced them to do so, whereupon Chief Oconostota made an ominous prediction.

"Brother, we have given you fine land," he said, "but I believe you will have much trouble settling it." The old chief's son, Dragging Canoe, added, "there is a dark cloud over the Country," meaning the Shawnees would be implacable enemies. Daniel didn't need to be reminded; the memory of James's battered body still haunted his dreams.

Nevertheless, on March 17, 1775, a treaty was signed, giving Henderson what he wanted. Ninety thousand square miles (233,100 square kilometers) became his for a mere $50,000. Only a month later, on April 19, 1775, 130 Minutemen (American patriots who were ready to serve on "a moment's notice") battled British troops on the road between Concord and Lexington in Massachusetts. The American Revolution wasn't a rumor anymore, it was a fact.

The Minutemen, a volunteer force of civilian militia, were ready "on a moment's notice" to serve the cause of the American Revolution.

Boone wasn't present at the treaty signing. He and thirty other men, including his brother Squire, were fifty miles (eighty kilometers) away. The woods rang with the sound of their axes as work commenced on a project called the Wilderness Road. Susannah, married less than a month, went along to cook for the crew.

Although the Warrior's Path had been used for generations by Indians, it remained a narrow trace (trail). To permit the passage of heavy settlers' wagons, it needed to be widened. Spring snows and freezing rains turned the job into backbreaking work, but for a few weeks there was no trouble from the Shawnees.

Then, when the road builders were only fifteen miles (twenty-four kilometers) from their destination at the edge of the Kentucky River, two woodcutters were badly wounded in a dawn attack and one was killed. A few days later, one of the wounded men died and at another camp, two men were found "killed and sculped." Boone informed Henderson by messenger. "If we give way to them [the Indians] now, it will ever be the case," he warned.

Henderson, following ten days behind Boone, replied by return messenger that he was hastening with reinforcements as fast as he could (The man who had carried Henderson's answer to Boone's request—none too eager to travel alone through Shawnee country—demanded ten thousand acres of Kentucky land as payment.)

Boone and Henderson started a settlement in a sloping, open meadow on the south side of the Kentucky River. Henderson named it Boonesborough in Daniel's honor. He drew up plans for a fort set farther back from the river, complete with blockhouses at each corner, stockade walls, and a well inside so that water would be available in case of an Indian siege.

It was time for Daniel to bring his family to their new home. Rebecca was expecting their ninth child. William, their eighth, born in the summer of 1775, had died soon after birth.

The fort at Boonesborough. The stockade walls and corner blockhouses were not completed until 1778, three years after Boone arrived in Kentucky.

After Rebecca recovered, the family began their journey to Kentucky, arriving at Boonesborough in the first week of September. From that time on, Daniel boasted that his wife and daughters were the first white women to stand on the banks of the Kentucky River.

In December 1775, Henderson's Transylvania Company opened for business, and nearly nine hundred land claims were filed. Daniel's was among the first, for a thousand acres southwest of Boonesborough along Tate's Creek. Without formal surveys, however, the boundaries of one settler's claim often overlapped the claim of another, creating a problem called "shingling."

Some settlers simply claimed land by "squatting" on it, making men afraid to go home for their families for fear someone would move into their cabins while they were gone. Just the same, Boonesborough took shape: a corn crop was planted, Squire Boone set up a gun shop, and a company store was opened.

FAR FROM HOME

Much has been written about how much Daniel Boone loved Kentucky. What was Rebecca's opinion? There wasn't a town, store, or church within three hundred miles. Boonesborough was a collection of rude cabins with floors of packed earth. Behind the cabins, the fort that was taking shape was a reminder that Indian attacks were expected. If Rebecca was dismayed, she kept it to herself.

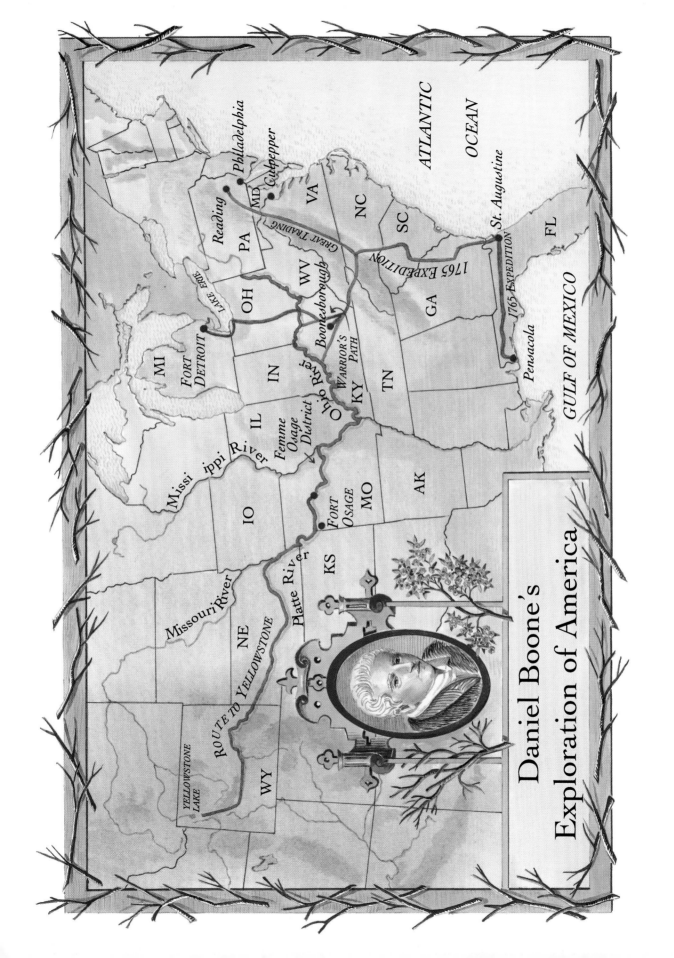

Daniel Boone's
Exploration of America

FIVE

Kidnapped in Kentucky

Sunday afternoon, July 14, 1776, was sunny and warm. Thirteen-year-old Jemima Boone and her friends Fanny and Betsey Callaway decided to pick flowers near the Kentucky River.

Daniel had warned everyone at Boonesborough not to wander far, but after a time the girls climbed into a canoe and amused themselves by paddling around in the water. Before they knew it, the current caught the canoe and took it downstream.

Across the river, three Shawnee and two Cherokee warriors were watching the girls. When the canoe got close to their side, they pulled it ashore and dragged their captives into the woods.

Nathan Reid and John Floyd, taking a Sunday stroll, heard the girls scream. Daniel was wakened from his Sunday nap and dashed barefooted to the river's edge. As the adults debated what to do, twelve-year-old John Gass jumped into the water, swam to the opposite shore,

Jemima Boone and the Callaway sisters, Fanny and Betsey, were kidnapped by Indians on July 14, 1776. The girls had only intended to take a ride in a canoe.

and brought the canoe back to the south side of the river. Then, as afternoon faded into evening, supplies were gathered for a rescue party.

Daniel found the Indians' trail, but soon it was too dark to see. The men, sick with fear about their daughters' fate, waited for daybreak to continue the search. They weren't the only ones up at dawn, though, and when the Indians discovered Betsey Callaway was digging the sharp heels of her leather shoes into the earth to mark a trail, the girls were given moccasins to wear. Even so, they managed to leave telltale signs along the way—a torn vine, a turned-over stone—so rescuers could follow them.

The second night the Indians made another "cold camp," one without a fire whose smoke or light would reveal their whereabouts. They traveled hard again the next day.

Daniel believed the kidnappers were headed for a river crossing at a place called Upper Blue Licks. He decided to head cross-country to intercept them.

When the Indians hadn't noticed any pursuers after three days, they became less cautious. They paused to hunt, roasted fresh meat over a fire, and invited the girls to share their meal. One of the warriors especially admired Jemima Boone's long black hair. He called her a fine-looking woman, though she was only thirteen.

After their meal, as the girls huddled together, Jemima glanced up to see her father creeping on his belly through the tall grass. A moment later shots rang out, and the Indians vanished into the woods. One of the rescuers, mistaking Betsey Callaway for an Indian, raised the butt of his rifle to smash her head.

"For God's sake," Daniel shouted, "don't kill her when we've traveled so far to save her!" Later it was learned that two of the Indians died of their wounds. One of them was the son of Blackfish, a Shawnee chief.

Jemima Boone said that the Indians had been "really kind to us," and she held no hatred for her captors. However, she vowed to obey her father's warnings in the future and promised to stay close by his side.

The girls' experience hastened a romance that had started before their capture. Three weeks after her kidnapping, Betsey Callaway married young Samuel Henderson, one of the men in the rescue party. Fifty years later, in 1826, the girls' harrowing story was immortalized by James Fenimore Cooper in his famous tale *The Last of the Mohicans*.

Only days after Betsey Callaway's wedding, news of the signing of the Declaration of Independence on July 4, 1776, reached Kentucky. Even such an important national event didn't capture the full attention of Kentuckians, however. They were more concerned about growing opposition to Richard Henderson's plan to establish a fourteenth colony.

Settlers resented the fact that Henderson doubled the price of land with some buyers, while selling large tracts to his friends at much lower prices. As early as 1775, when the Continental Congress met in Philadelphia, Thomas Jefferson and John Adams had noted that the territory purchased by Henderson belonged to Virginia and North Carolina according to their charters, which they agreed should take precedence over Henderson's claims.

Daniel Boone and other men from Boonesborough rescued the girls, who were unharmed. However, two of the Indians were killed when their camp was raided.

How Boone Became Famous

John Filson, a thirty-four-year-old Pennsylvania schoolteacher, spent the summer of 1783 with Daniel Boone. The following year he published a book about Kentucky, containing a thirty-three-page appendix titled "The Adventures of Col. Daniel Boon." Boone's name was misspelled, but his exploits—written as if by his own hand—made the book a success in America. It created a sensation in England, then was translated into French and German. Filson didn't live to enjoy his success; he was killed by Indians in 1788.

In 1776, the Virginia General Assembly resolved that land could not be bought from the Indians without the colony's approval. In effect, the Sycamore Shoals agreement was voided. Daniel never received the two thousand acres of fine bluegrass land he'd been promised. However, his youngest son, Nathan, recalled that it was not his father's nature to brood about matters he couldn't change.

While the American Revolution raged on, settlers in Kentucky fought a different war. Chief Blackfish, whose son had been killed during the rescue of the three girls, ordered attacks on Kentucky settlements, including Boonesborough. When a militia was called up, it was not to fight the British, but to defend settlers against Indian raids.

In March 1777, Blackfish began his first assault on Boonesborough, which resulted in the death of a slave. Then, on a quiet morning in April, when the cows were let out of the fort to go to pasture, they refused to budge. Boone sent two men from the fort to investigate. They could find no reason for the cows' contrariness, but as they returned to the fort they were fired on by several Shawnees.

In the melee that followed, Daniel yelled to his companions, "Boys, we'll have to fight for it—sell your lives dear!" He was hit in the ankle. The wound was slow to heal and plagued him the rest of his life.

The Declaration of Independence, written almost entirely by Thomas Jefferson, was adopted on July 4, 1776.

Blackfish failed in that attempt to drive the whites out of Boones-borough, but he destroyed their corn crop and made it hard for them to hunt for fresh game. With meat in short supply, settlers gathered nuts and grapes from the forest to tide them over. The well inside the fort had never been finished, so rainwater had to be collected in barrels.

The settlers ran low on salt, an important preservative in a day when refrigeration was unheard-of. In January 1778, Boone decided to take a party of thirty men to salt springs near the Licking River several miles from the fort. The Indians weren't likely to make war in the deep of winter, he reasoned, but would be staying warm beside their own fires.

Today, we buy salt in convenient containers from grocery stores, but "making salt" in long-ago times was hard work. The salt springs where Boone and his men set up camp produced several thousand gallons of brine (salt water) each day. It took 840 gallons (381 kilograms) to make one bushel (.036 cubic meters) of salt, which was obtained by boiling down the brine in heavy iron kettles, then scraping up the salt crystals.

On a cold February day, as the men tended the kettles, Daniel left camp to check some beaver traps he'd set ten miles (sixteen kilometers) away. Along the way, he killed a buffalo. He butchered the animal on the spot and loaded four hundred pounds (180 kilograms) of meat onto his horse, lashing it in place with rawhide thongs. Evening fell and it started to snow as Daniel led his mount back to the salt camp.

Suddenly an uneasy feeling seized him. A glance over his shoulder told Daniel that a party of Shawnees was sneaking up behind him. He tried to slip the load of meat off the horse and mount up, but it was frozen in place. He tried to cut it loose, but his bloody knife was frozen inside its sheath. Daniel took a deep breath. He'd have to make a run for it.

SIX

You Will Be the First to Die

The Shawnee warriors were vigorous young men; Daniel was forty-four years old. The salt camp was ten miles away. He knew he couldn't outrun them. After half a mile, he stopped, leaned his rifle against a tree as a sign of surrender, and faced his pursuers.

The Shawnees took charge of the horse and meat, then hustled their prisoner through the winter darkness to Chief Blackfish's camp. What Boone discovered when they arrived surprised him.

Indians didn't usually go against an enemy in the winter, but more than a hundred braves had painted their faces red for war. The notorious Girty brothers, George and James—called "white Indians" because they had taken up Indian ways—were in camp. Another surprise was the presence of an escaped slave, Pompey, who acted as an interpreter for the Shawnees.

Daniel was hauled before Blackfish. The chief demanded to know

The Shawnees were proud warriors. The warrior pictured here was sometimes called "the Prophet."

why Boone and his men were at the salt lick. To make salt, Boone replied honestly.

Blackfish told Daniel that to avenge the death of Chief Cornstalk, who had been murdered by whites in Virginia after signing a peace treaty with them in 1774, the Shawnees planned to destroy all settlements along the Kentucky River. The first deaths Blackfish had in mind were Boone's and the saltmakers'.

Boone warned that although the Shawnees outnumbered the saltmakers, a confrontation would be bloody—Indians would die too.

BLACKS ON THE FRONTIER

Escaped slaves often found safe havens in Indian villages. As people of color themselves, many tribes were inclined to accept blacks as equals. When Lewis and Clark went up the Missouri River in 1804, the Arikaras (who had never seen a black person before) greatly admired York, Clark's servant, who let them try to rub the color off his skin. Blacks also played important roles—both as slaves and as free men—in western settlements. At Boonesborough, a black man named Uncle Monk was respected as a superior hunter, blacksmith and musician.

Daniel had a different suggestion; later it would become the basis of a charge of treason against him.

Daniel told Blackfish he would ask the saltmakers to surrender peacefully. He pointed out that the men were more valuable alive than dead: The Shawnees could keep them as slaves or sell them to the British for a bounty. Then, when spring came, he would take Blackfish to Boonesborough and ask everyone at the fort to surrender, too.

Blackfish was pleased with the proposition. He conferred with his warriors, who also agreed to Boone's plan.

The next day, the Shawnees headed for the salt springs. Blackfish told Daniel to enter camp first, warning that if the saltmakers put up a fight, "You will be the first to die."

Two of the saltmakers had gone hunting, as Daniel himself had the day before. The sight of Boone, followed by a party of painted warriors, caused the men who remained to grab their rifles.

"Don't fire!" Daniel yelled. "If you do, we'll all be massacred!" But after the men laid down their weapons, many of the Indians changed their minds: they wanted to kill the saltmakers on the spot. Daniel was given a chance to plead their case, with Pompey translating.

"Brothers!" Daniel cried. "To kill [these men] would displease the Great Spirit. . . . If you spare them they will make you fine warriors, and excellent hunters to kill game for your squaws and children."

Again Blackfish counseled with his warriors. After a heated argument, they agreed to spare the saltmakers' lives—by a vote of fifty-nine for death, sixty-one for life. For now, the prisoners wouldn't have to "run the gauntlet," a Shawnee custom.

Except for Boone, that is.

Perhaps because Daniel was the leader of the group, Blackfish ordered him to run for his life. This meant sprinting between two lines of warriors six feet (two meters) apart, armed with sticks, stones, clubs, and prods made of deer antlers. If a man fell, he was usually beaten to death.

Daniel was stripped nearly naked. Then he zigzagged down the gauntlet, dodging blows as best he could. A kick from a warrior almost knocked him to his knees, a whack from a club cut a deep gash in his scalp, but he made it to the end alive. The saltmakers cheered, as did the Indians, who admired courage no matter what a man's color.

Then began a cold hundred-mile (160-kilometer), ten-day march to the Indians' permanent camp east of present-day Dayton, Ohio. When bad weather kept the Shawnees from finding game, they killed their dogs for food. When they arrived on February 18, 1778, it was the other saltmakers' turn to run the gauntlet, and one ended up with a broken arm. Afterward the Shawnees celebrated with a war dance. For entertainment, they made the whites dance too.

Many of Daniel's men regretted surrendering at the salt camp. Even though the Indians had voted to spare them, most believed they'd be killed eventually. They didn't realize that the Shawnees had a practical reason for letting them live.

The adoption of white captives was a common practice in many tribes. When word got around that Blackfish had several prisoners, Indian visitors came to check them out as potential sons, brothers, or slaves. Blackfish had already made his choice: he picked Daniel Boone. Before the adoption took place, however, Blackfish asked Daniel about his role in the search party that had rescued Jemima and the Callaway sisters. Daniel admitted he'd been the leader of that party. Yes, he added, it might have been his shot that killed the chief's son. "Many things happen in war," he reminded Blackfish. After a moment of reflection, the chief agreed that it was so.

The Shawnees had a special ritual designed to make a white man suitable for adoption. The women of the tribe took Daniel to the river—it was March and still bitterly cold—and stripped him to his skin. They scrubbed him with sand and pebbles until his flesh was raw, to "take all his white blood out." His hair was plucked out (a painful process!), except for a lock on the top of his head. He was given Indian clothing, a feast was held, and he was given a new name. Henceforth, he would be called Sheltowee, or Big Turtle.

Sixteen of the other saltmakers were also adopted. Two of them formed lasting friendships with the Shawnees; when Jack Dunn was later captured by Kentucky militiamen, he was executed as a traitor. The men who were not adopted—the Indians called them "no-goods"—were taken to Fort Detroit and sold to the British for twenty pounds each.

LIFE & TIMES OF COL. DANIEL BOONE.

BOONE'S INDIAN TOILETTE, PAGE 182.

After his capture by the Shawnees in 1778, Daniel Boone was adopted by Chief Blackfish. He followed Indian customs and even took a new name, Sheltowee, or Big Turtle. Later, Boone was charged with treason for being too friendly with the Indians.

Daniel accompanied Blackfish to Fort Detroit. The British governor, Henry Hamilton, knew of Boone's reputation and believed he'd make a fine secret agent for the Loyalists. He offered Blackfish one hundred pounds for him, but the chief refused. He said he had come to love Boone too well to part with him. Nevertheless, hoping that Boone would eventually come over to the British side, Hamilton gave him several presents—

a horse, a saddle, a bridle, and a blanket. The gifts embittered some of Boone's men, who suspected him of double-dealing.

When Flanders Callaway and Thomas Brooks returned to the salt camp, they searched for clues to the fate of their missing friends. Moccasin tracks in the snow told them what had happened. They hurried back to Boonesborough and reported that the saltmakers had been captured "without Shedding one drop of blood."

Rebecca Boone didn't know if she was a widow or not. She waited two months for Daniel's return, then went back to North Carolina. Fifteen-year-old Jemima stayed on at Boonesborough with her new husband, Flanders Callaway. Two years earlier, she'd been sure that Daniel would rescue her. Now she prayed he could save himself.

Daniel's fellow prisoners were disgusted by how quickly their leader adjusted to Indian life. Blackfish and his wife were delighted with their new son, and Boone didn't hide the fact that he was fond of their two daughters, two and five years of age. Daniel said later that he was treated with respect by the Shawnees. It didn't mean he wanted to remain a prisoner longer than necessary, but there was no way he could explain that to his men for fear word might get back to Blackfish.

Instead, Daniel took pains to seem contented. He whistled as he worked. He participated in Indian games (careful to let the warriors win more often than he did), and was allowed to hunt with the Shawnees. Blackfish rationed the gunpowder he gave Daniel, however, and often sent his daughters to spy on Boone.

In June 1778, the Indians moved to a salt spring near the Scioto River. Daniel helped them make salt, using the very kettles the Indians had taken from his own camp. All the while, he hoarded food and gunpowder and kept an eye peeled for a chance to slip unnoticed into the forest.

One afternoon, four months after his capture, a flock of turkeys flew out of the woods near the Indian camp. Shawnee hunters pursued them, leaving Daniel behind with the women and children. It was the chance he'd been waiting for. He gathered up everything he'd collected—dried venison, gunpowder, and a rifle he'd assembled piece by piece when he was asked to repair the Indians' weapons.

He ran to his horse. Blackfish's wife wept, warning that he'd be killed when he was caught. Daniel admitted later that his Shawnee mother's tears touched his heart, but he took off at a hard gallop.

To make it difficult for the Shawnees to track him, Daniel rode his horse in the beds of creeks. When the horse wore out, he turned it loose and took off on foot, covering 160 miles (260 kilometers) in four days.

When he arrived at Boonesborough on June 20, 1778, his feet swollen and blistered, he hurried straight to his cabin. His wife, children, household possessions—all were gone! Only the family cat remained. But when word reached Jemima that Daniel had returned, she ran to meet him and threw her arms around his neck. Her prayers had been answered.

SEVEN

Two Sons and a Brother

Not everyone was pleased to see Daniel again.

Stories about the surrender of the saltmakers had circulated through the settlements, and many people believed Daniel was a traitor. Rumors about how he'd enjoyed Indian life—even that he had taken an Indian wife—raised questions about his loyalty.

Nevertheless, he was in charge of Boonesborough, and as soon as he recovered from his flight through the woods, he realized that the fort was in no shape to repel a Shawnee attack. The stockade fence was in disrepair; the well inside the fort hadn't been finished; food supplies were low. Boone set every man and woman to work, even calling on Harrodsburg and Logan's Station for help.

A month later, another saltmaker escaped from Blackfish's camp. After Boone got away, the Indians had watched their captives like hawks. William Hancock's adoptive father even took his "son's" clothes

Before the siege of Boonesborough, in September 1778, Daniel Boone set everyone to work repairing the stockade fence, gathering food, and finishing the well.

away each night. Hancock took off anyway, arriving home nine days later as naked as a baby. He confirmed Daniel's suspicions: the Shawnees planned an all-out assault on Boonesborough and would be accompanied by British soldiers.

September 7, 1778, dawned warm and clear. The meadow in front of the fort was deserted. Women fetched water from the river while boys fed the livestock. Daniel and others patrolled the area for signs of the enemy. At midmorning, four hundred Indians, mostly Shawnees, and a handful of French-Canadian and British troops were seen coming down the ridge. Raising a white flag, Pompey, Blackfish's interpreter, approached the fort and announced that Blackfish had a letter from the lieutenant governor, Henry Hamilton.

When Daniel stepped outside, many were sure he'd be killed. Others feared he'd surrender them just as he'd given up the saltmakers.

Blackfish's eyes filled with tears as he called Boone by his Indian name, Sheltowee, and asked why he'd run away. Daniel answered that he'd gotten lonesome for his wife and children. Blackfish reminded him of his promise to hand over the fort peacefully, but Daniel stalled for time. When the chief said his warriors were hungry, Daniel invited Blackfish to kill some cattle and gather corn from the settlers' fields.

Inside the fort, the settlers were divided about what to do next. Half the men believed they ought to surrender; the others—including Daniel's brother Squire—vowed to fight to their deaths. After a discussion, all agreed to fight. Daniel, who had been willing to continue negotiating with the enemy, said he'd "die with the rest."

In a scuffle with the Indians a few days later, Daniel got a tomahawk gash on the head and Squire was hit in the shoulder as they ran back to the shelter of the fort. During the siege, Jemima was lightly wounded, too. The Shawnees tried to burn down the fort by setting fire to bundles of flax that were stored near the stockade walls. That didn't work, so flaming arrows were shot over the walls, which the settlers doused in buckets of water. The Indians had been digging a tunnel toward the fort and were within twenty feet of the stockade walls when it began to rain heavily, collapsing the tunnel.

On September 17, the settlers noticed that all was quiet outside. The longest siege in Kentucky history—ten days of torment—had ended. Two men had been lost and four wounded. The Indians had lost thirty-seven; among them was Pompey.

The siege was hardly over when Daniel found himself charged with

treason by Richard Callaway and Benjamin Logan. They accused him of being too friendly with Blackfish, taking an Indian wife, not trying hard enough to escape from the Shawnees, and bargaining with the British governor at Fort Detroit.

Boone faced his accusers squarely. The only reason he had surrendered the saltmakers, he explained, was to save their lives, as well as the lives of those at the fort, who were not prepared to fend off an Indian attack.

The court-martial ruled in Daniel's favor, but the criticism and suspicion had worn him down. He left for North Carolina in November 1778, and found Rebecca living in a small cabin near her relatives. She wasn't eager to return to Kentucky, but as fear mounted about the out-

Blackfish's forces confront Daniel Boone at Boonesborough.

come of the American Revolution, she agreed it would be wise to leave.

In September 1779, the Boones and many of Rebecca's relatives headed back to Kentucky. They arrived in October, but Boonesborough was a very different place from what it had been just a year before. It bustled with new settlers, a school had been started, and the best corn crop ever had been harvested.

Whether it was because he harbored bad memories about his trial, or because the throng of new settlers made him feel hemmed in, Daniel moved six miles (ten kilometers) away and started a new settlement, Boone's Station (near present-day Athens, Kentucky). His household was larger than ever—it now included the six orphaned children of one of Rebecca's brothers.

In addition to raising cattle, corn, and tobacco, Daniel became a land speculator. When two friends gave him money—said to be between forty and fifty thousand dollars—to help file land claims, he was robbed of every penny while staying at a back-country inn in Virginia. He vowed to pay it back—and did—but it took him to the end of his life. The Shawnees, spurred on by the British, had not given up their attacks on white settlements. Boone became a scout for General George Rogers Clark as he pursued the Shawnee in Ohio.

Ned Boone was killed in a skirmish with the Indians in October 1780. The Shawnees were gleeful. Because Ned looked so much like Daniel, they believed they'd killed the man they called Wide Mouth. To Daniel's lasting grief, they beheaded Ned and paraded the trophy through their villages.

At the time, Kentucky was the westernmost county of Virginia, so its official business was conducted through the Virginia General Assembly in Williamsburg. In November 1780, Kentucky itself was divided into three counties. Daniel became a lieutenant colonel in the Fayette County militia, then a county sheriff the following year. He was also elected to the General Assembly as a representative from Fayette County. When he went to take his seat, dressed in the leather leggings of a woodsman, British soldiers along the way took him into custody. Boone convinced them he was a common farmer doing a farmer's business, and was released. Meantime, Rebecca had her hands full, too. Already a grandmother, she gave birth in March 1781 to her tenth and last child, a son, Nathan.

In a fierce battle with the British and Indians at Blue Licks in late 1782, Daniel's twenty-three-year-old son Israel fought by his side. The young man, though ill with fever, had gotten out of bed to join the militia. His father caught a riderless horse and urged his son to mount up and go home, but Israel vowed to fight on. Moments later he was shot

Daniel Boone lost his son Israel at the Battle of Blue Licks in 1782.
It was a sad time, for he'd already lost his oldest son, James, in 1773.

through the neck. Before Daniel could reach him, Israel's eyes were glazed in death. It was another low point in Boone's life: he'd lost two beloved sons to the Indians, James and Israel, as well as his brother Ned.

In November 1782, the Americans and British began peace negotiations. Daniel was almost fifty years old, and welcomed the prospect of a new beginning. The Treaty of Paris in 1783 formally ended the colonists' rebellion against the British. The American Revolution was over at last.

In 1783, the Boones moved to Limestone, Kentucky, where Daniel became a tavernkeeper, a surveyor, and a horse trader. He acquired 100,000 acres of land, making him among the wealthiest men in Kentucky. But as always, trouble with claims plagued him. Often the fault was his, because he neglected to follow through with paperwork that would guarantee ownership. Years later, he said his claims were swallowed up "through my own ignorance."

Boone had fought Indians, blazed a road through the wilderness, rescued three kidnapped girls, and escaped from the Shawnees. He'd proved his mettle, but he was no match for lawyers. Fresh suits were filed against him; acre by acre, he lost his lands again.

Kentucky became a state in 1792, with a population of 75,000. Daniel, fifty-seven years old, was troubled by rheumatism and vexed that civilization was gaining on him faster than he could outrun it. With most of his land gone and game harder than ever to find, he decided to try his luck elsewhere.

The territory of Missouri—where Daniel's son, Daniel Morgan Boone, had settled in 1795—was the newest land of promise. When the last acre of his Kentucky claims was taken for taxes, Boone left Kentucky. In September 1799—the year George Washington died—Daniel Boone once again turned his eyes westward.

Rebecca, the Boone daughters Jemima and Susannah, their husbands, eighteen-year-old Nathan, and thirty-year-old son Daniel Morgan accompanied Daniel. So did his brother Squire and several other families who'd also lost their claims. Traveling by canoe, horseback, and wagon, they arrived in Missouri in October 1799. Family legend has it that Daniel walked every step of the way. His feet were old, but they still itched.

EIGHT

Leave the Rest to History

In 1799, St. Louis was a rough-and-tumble town of nearly five hundred people, mostly French. Boone's reputation had preceded him, and he was warmly welcomed.

The governor of the region appointed Daniel a "syndic," or administrator, for the Femme Osage district, and granted him 850 acres of land. Daniel built a log home—it would be his last. Squire Boone settled several miles away, but soon returned to Kentucky.

Game was plentiful, so Daniel and Nathan hunted deer for their hides, worth about forty cents each, compared to a dollar in the old days. Beaver pelts fetched three dollars, meaning a man could still make a decent living.

After a few months in Missouri, Daniel was appointed a district sheriff and judge. He held court under a large elm tree near his home, delivering justice that was rough but fair. When a squabble arose

Daniel Boone traveled west a final time in 1799 and settled with his family not far from St. Louis, Missouri.

between a poor widow and a farmer over a cow, the farmer had the stronger case, so Daniel ruled in his favor. The next case involved a chronic troublemaker, but rather than lock the fellow up, Daniel decreed that he must give the widow in the previous case a cow to replace the one she'd lost.

The Louisiana Purchase, signed in Paris by the United States and France on April 30, 1803, changed the history of the west: 800,000 square miles (2,072,000 square kilometers) of land were transferred to the United States, doubling the size of the nation. The western frontier was moved from the banks of the Mississippi River all the way to the Rocky Mountains.

Within a year, the French governors in St. Louis were replaced by American commissioners. As usual, Daniel had failed to certify the boundaries of the land granted to him by the French. In 1804, American officials denied the validity of his claims. Once again, Daniel was stripped of his property.

All his life, Daniel Boone was most at home in a land that wasn't yet settled, where game was still abundant and neighbors weren't too near.

In Missouri, a settler's cabin was much like those in the other regions where Daniel and Rebecca Boone had settled—and the work of felling trees, growing crops, and finding game was just as hard.

As Missouri filled up with immigrants, Daniel—who still craved the solitude of unpopulated fields and forests—found himself with neighbors close on all sides. But he was seventy years old; it was too late to make another new start.

Instead, he settled down to hunt, fish, and even make salt, as he'd done thirty years before. At Brine Springs in Howard County, Missouri, Daniel, Daniel Morgan, and Nathan set up a salt camp that became known as Boone's Lick, hired six men to operate it, and shipped salt upriver to St. Louis.

Rebecca worked as hard as ever, making hundreds of gallons of maple syrup each spring, which she sold. On a bright day in 1813, she went to the woods to boil sap. She returned early, saying she didn't feel well, and died on March 18, at age seventy-four. She was buried on a bluff overlooking the Missouri River. Daniel's wandering had kept him from Rebecca's side for most of their married life, but many said he "was never contented again" after her death.

For a time it seemed as if Boone might not die landless after all. In February 1814, President James Madison supported a special act of Congress honoring Daniel with an award of 850 acres of land in

To the end of his life, Daniel Boone was happiest when he could explore the woods and fields with a hunting rifle in his hand and a good dog at his side.

Missouri. When his old debtors in Kentucky heard of it, they presented Daniel with claims more than twenty years old. He was forced to sell off every acre he'd been granted. He had explored more of the West than any man of his day, but died without owning any of it.

Age didn't mean Daniel intended to stay put. He explored the plains of Kansas, Dakota Territory, and the Yellowstone country of Wyoming. He made it all the way to the foot of the Rockies and spoke of getting to California someday.

In 1810, Daniel returned to Kentucky to visit his brother Squire. Along the way he met a stranger whose actions struck him as peculiar. The young man wasn't shooting birds and animals—he was painting their likenesses on paper. The stranger introduced himself—John James Audubon—and the sketches he made of Boone at that time are among the few portraits we have of him today.

Daniel made a final visit to Kentucky in 1817 to pay off his last debts there. When he got back to Missouri, he had fifty cents left in his pocket.

Daniel realized—perhaps with astonishment—that he was an old man. His sight had failed—now when he went hunting and trapping he stayed in camp to cook for his sons and grandsons. What a great blessing were all those grandchildren—fifty-two of them nearby, others scattered farther away.

After news came that Squire had died, Daniel felt his own end approaching. He supervised the building of a cherrywood casket for himself, and joked that he'd "taken many a nice nap in it."

On September 23, 1820, Daniel came down with a fever after visiting Jemima, who had vowed at thirteen never to stray far from his side—and returned to Nathan's house. He died on the morning of September 26, a month short of his eighty-sixth birthday. The local minister performed a simple service, calling Daniel "a good man," and suggested that "the rest be left to history."

John James Audubon met Daniel Boone quite by chance as both were walking through the Kentucky woods in 1810. Audubon made several sketches and later painted this portrait of the frontiersman.

Even death didn't stop Daniel's wandering ways. Twenty-five years after his passing, Kentucky and Missouri feuded about who owned Daniel's bones. Finally, both Daniel and Rebecca were reburied in Frankfort, Kentucky, the state capital. But an expert in identifying such remains wasn't sure the bones assumed to be Daniel's were actually his. It seems a fitting end for a man to whom something beyond the mountains always whispered.

Daniel Boone and His Times

1681 King George II grants William Penn, a Quaker, 28 million acres of land in New World

1682 Penn founds Philadelphia

1712 Squire Boone, Daniel's father, comes to America

1717 George Boone, Daniel's Quaker grandfather, settles in Oley Township in Pennsylvania

1720 Squire Boone marries Sarah Morgan

1734 Daniel Boone born on November 2

1750 Boone family moves to North Carolina after dispute with fellow Quakers

1754 Daniel meets fifteen-year-old Rebecca Bryan

1755 Daniel volunteers for militia; becomes wagoner in "Braddock's War"; meets John Findley

1756 Daniel marries Rebecca Bryan on August 14

1757 Boones' first son, James, is born

1759 Daniel moves his family to Virginia

1763 Spain cedes Florida to Britain; one hundred acres of free land offered to Protestant settlers

1765 Daniel leads party of explorers to Florida; Daniel's father dies

1768 John Findley visits Daniel; tells stories about *Kan-ta-ke* (Kentucky)

Daniel Boone and His Times

1769 Boone locates the Cumberland Gap

1773 Daniel's oldest son, James, killed in Indian ambush

1775 Daniel builds Wilderness Road; American Revolution begins

1776 Declaration of Independence adopted; Jemima Boone and Callaway sisters are kidnapped by Shawnees

1778 Daniel and saltmakers are captured by Shawnees; Daniel is adopted by Chief Blackfish; Boonesborough is besieged; court-martial clears Boone of treason

1780 Ned Boone is killed and beheaded by Shawnees

1781 Rebecca gives birth to Boones' tenth and last child

1782 Daniel fights in Battle of Blue Licks; son Israel is killed

1783 Daniel becomes tavernkeeper and land dealer; peace treaty is signed in Paris, ending Revolutionary War

1788 U.S. Constitution ratified in Philadelphia

1792 Kentucky becomes fifteenth state

1799 Boone family heads west to Missouri; George Washington dies

1800 French appoint Daniel as syndic at Femme Osage district near St. Louis; U.S. capital moved from Philadelphia to Washington, D.C.

1803 Thomas Jefferson buys Louisiana Territory (800,000 square miles or 2,072,000 square kilometers) from France for $15,000,000

1804 Lewis and Clark begin journey up Missouri River

1808 U.S. outlaws importation of slaves from Africa; slavery itself remains legal

1812 Second war between Britain and America erupts

1813 Death of Rebecca Boone, age seventy-four

1817 Boone makes last trip to Kentucky, pays off old debts

1820 Daniel Boone dies in Missouri on September 26, a month shy of
eighty-sixth birthday

Further Research

Books

Cavan, Seamus. *Daniel Boone and the Opening of the Ohio Country.* New York: Chelsea House Publishers, 1991.

Cobblestone, *The History Magazine for Young People: Daniel Boone.* Volume 9, no. 6, June 1988. (Issue devoted to Boone, his life and times.)

Hargrove, Jim. *Daniel Boone: Pioneer Trailblazer.* Chicago: Children's Press, 1985.

Lawlor, Laurie: *Daniel Boone.* Niles, IL: Albert Whitman, 1989.

Sanford, William R. and Carl R. Green. *Daniel Boone: Wilderness Pioneer.* Springfield, NJ: Enslow Publishers, 1997.

Websites

Daniel Boone
http://www.americanwest.com/pages/boone.htm

Daniel Boone
Myth and Reality in American Consciousness
http://xroads.virginia.edu/~HYPER/HNS/smithhome.html

Bibliography

Alvord, Clarence W. "The Daniel Boone Myth." *Journal of the Illinois State Historical Society*, Apr-July 1926, p. 19.

Amyx, Clifford. "The Authentic Image of Daniel Boone." *Missouri Historical Review*, 82:2, Jan 1988, p. 153.

Bakeless, John. *Daniel Boone.* Harrisburg, PA: Stackpole Company, 1965.

Butterfield, Conrad W. *History of the Girtys.* Cincinnati, OH: Robert Clarke, 1890.

Calvert, Patricia. Great Lives: *The American West.* New York: Atheneum, 1997.

Chitwood, Oliver P.: *A History of Colonial America.* New York: Harper and Brothers, 1931.

Comfort, William W. *The Quakers: A Brief Account of Their Influence on Pennsylvania.* Gettysburg: Pennsylvania Historial Association, 1948.

Doherty, Kieran. *William Penn: Quaker Colonist.* Brookfield, CT: Millbrook Press, 1998.

Draper, Lyman Copeland. *Draper's Life of Boone: Series B.* Madison, WI: The State Historical Society, 1983.

————. *The Daniel Boone Papers: Series C.* Madison, WI: The State Historical Society, 1983.

Elliott, Lawrence. *The Long Hunter: A New Life of Daniel Boone.* New York: Reader's Digest Press, 1976.

Fantel, Hans. *William Penn: Apostle of Dissent.* New York: William Morrow, 1974.

Faragher, John M. *Daniel Boone: The Life and Legend of an American Pioneer.* New York: Henry Holt, 1992.

Hammon, Neal O. "*The Legend of Daniel Boone's Cabin at Harrodsburg.*" *Filson Club History Quarterly*, 1974, 48:241.

Bibliography

Herrick, Francis H. *Audubon the Naturalist: A History of His Life and Times.* New York: D. Appleton, 1917.

Hurt, R. Douglas. *Nathan Boone and the American Frontier.* Columbia, MO: University of Missouri Press, 1998.

Lester, William S. *The Transylvania Company.* Spencer, IN: Samuel R. Guard and Co., 1935.

Lofaro, Michael A. *The Life and Adventures of Daniel Boone.* Lexington, KY: University Press of Kentucky, 1986.

Spraker, Hazel Atterbury. *The Boone Family: A Genealogical History of the Descendants of George and Mary Boone.* Baltimore: Genealogical Publishing Co., Inc., 1977.

Walton, John. "Ghost Writer to Daniel Boone." *American Heritage*, Oct 1955, p. 10.

Source Notes

Chapter 1:

p. 9: "above all her children": John M. Faragher, *Daniel Boone: The Life and Legend of an American Pioneer* (Henry Holt, 1992), p. 13.

p. 9: "Canst thou not beg?": Faragher, p. 13.

p. 10: "Daniel was ever unpracticed...": John Bakeless, *Daniel Boone* (Stackpole, 1965), p. 10.

p. 11: "be more Careful for the future": Bakeless, p. 16.

p. 13: "The Boones were wanderers born. . . ": Bakeless, p. 5.

p. 14: "settle down. . . ": Lawrence Elliott, *The Long Hunter: A New Life of Daniel Boone* (Reader's Digest Press, 1976), p. 21.

Chapter 2:

p. 18: "little courage and no good will": Patricia Calvert, *Great Lives: The American West* (Atheneum, 1997), p. 3.

p. 19: "colors flying, drums beating. . . ": Lyman Copeland Draper, *Draper's Life of Boone: Series B* (Wisconsin State Historical Society, 1983), p. 45.

p. 19: "like sheep before the hounds":Calvert, p. 3.

p. 20: "a good gun, a good horse, and a good wife": Bakeless, p. 30.

Chapter 3:

p. 24: "Dry up your tears": Faragher, p. 59.

Chapter 4:

p. 31: "hugging the little fellow . . .": Draper, 6S41-42

p. 32: "James was a good son. . . ": *Michael A. Lofaro, The Life and Adventures of Daniel Boone* (University Press of Kentucky, 1986), p. 74.

p. 32: "the worst melancholy of my life": Laurie Lawlor, *Daniel Boone* (Albert Whitman, 1989), p. 67.

p. 32: "two of the best Hands . . .": Faragher, p. 100.

p. 34: "Brother, we have given you a fine land. . . ": Faragher, p. 112.

p. 34: "there is a dark cloud over the Country": Faragher, p. 112.

p. 36: "killed and sculped". . . "If we give way to them now. . . ": Lofaro, p. 46.

Chapter 5:

p. 42: "For God's sake, don't kill her. . . ": Faragher, p. 137.

p. 42: "really kind to us": Faragher, p. 140.

p. 45: "Boys, we'll have to fight for it. . . ": Lawlor, p. 99.

Chapter 6:

p. 50: "You will be the first to die.": Faragher, p. 158.

p. 50: "Don't fire!": Faragher, p. 158.

p. 50: "Brothers!...": Lawlor, p. 105.

p. 51: "Many things happen in war": Faragher, p. 165.

p. 51: "take all his white blood out": Bakeless, p. 177.

Source Notes

p. 53: "without Shedding one drop of blood": Bakeless, p. 169.

Chapter 7:
p. 57: "die with the rest": Lofaro, p. 81.
p, 62: "through my own ignorance": Lofaro, p. 108.
p. 62: "was never contented again": Calvert, p. 13.

Chapter 8:
p. 68: "taken many a nice nap in it": Faragher, p. 316.
p. 69: "a good man" . . . "the rest be left to history": Elliott, p. 203.

Index

Page numbers in boldface are illustrations.

Index

EPSOM PUBLIC LIBRARY

1893